Ghost Stories from the Historical Archives

Scottish Paranormal

Book 1

All rights reserved. This book, or parts thereof, may not be reproduced or transmitted in any form or by any means, electronic or mechanical, including printing, recording, photocopying or by any information storage and retrieval system without written permission from the author.

This book is written in British English

ISBN: 9798614403799

© Scottish Paranormal
© Gregor Stewart

2020

Contents

Introduction	4
The Poltergeist of Pitmilly	5
The Green Lady of Fernie	8
The Headless Horseman of Stonehaven	10
The White Lady of St Andrews	13
The Handless Girl of Rait Castle	16
Lady Crawford of Springfield	19
The Grey Lady of Burleigh Castle	21
The Witch of Abergeldie	23
The Secretive Ghost of Rossend Castle	26
The Curse of Alloa Tower	29
The Shadow-Man of Newark Castle	34
The Curious Case of St Monans Church	36
The Green Lady of Ashintully	39
The Phantom Monk of Balmerino	43
The Giant Piper of Cortachy Castle	45
The Whistling Wraith of Balcomie Castle	49
The Sad Tale of Castle Grant	52
The Tale of 'Bluidy Bruce'	55
The Spectral Sailor of The Glenlee	57
The Smothered Piper of St Andrews	60
The Dark Monk of Fidra	62
The Mackie Poltergeist	65
The Disaster at the Old Kirk	69
The Murdered Lord of Inchdrewer	71
The Tragedy at Kellie Castle	75
The Phantom Vikings of Iona	77
The Cursed Necklace of Loch Leven	80
About Scottish Paranormal	84

Introduction

Scottish Paranormal are one of the oldest paranormal research teams in Scotland. Having investigated extensively throughout the UK, and further afield, we have gathered a vast number of tales of alleged hauntings.

Our research into these stories is always heavily history based, we firmly believe that for there to be a haunting, there has to be a reason, and that reason lies in the historical records. By doing this research, we are able to being the full story together, and often find the history is a more interesting story than that which has been passed down and changed through the generations.

Here, for the first time, the team bring together a collection of some of their favourite ghost stories from across Scotland, including iconic locations and famous figures with tales of deceit, double-crossing, murder and mystery.

We do hope that you enjoy our choice of stories. For further details regarding Scottish Paranormal and to be kept up to date with our future projects, please see the final chapter of the book.

The Poltergeist of Pitmilly

While most readers will have read about cases such as the Sauchie Poltergeist or the Enfield Poltergeist, the Pitmilly Poltergeist is sadly predominantly forgotten, despite it being one of the strongest and most convincing cases in history.

Pitmilly House stood around 5 miles outside St Andrews, close to the village of Kingsbarns. Dating back to medieval times, with a later wing added during the Georgian Era, Pitmilly House was home to the Monypenny family for over 7 centuries until, in 1930, it was purchased by Captain J.A. Jeffrey, who moved there with his family and 2 maids. Their family life was happy until an event in 1936, which would signify the start of one of the longest running poltergeist cases in history. As the family sat around the dining table eating a meal, a piece of burning coal suddenly appeared above the table before it dropped, landing in the centre of the table and sending the family running to extinguish it before the table caught fire. It was only then that they could take stock of what had happened, and the question of how the burning coal could appear above the table.

In 1940, the house suffered extensive fire damage, and the fire service report revealed the terrifying reality of what was going on. They reported that there was between 8 or 9 seats of fire, each one in a different room and each one starting just below the ceiling level. It would have been physically impossible for the fire to have been started in this manner, and thoughts turned to whether it had been more incidents of lumps of burning coal appearing.

The ruins of the stables and stores are all that survive of Pitmilly House

Extensive investigations were carried out into the cause, and while they concluded that there was no human causes behind the fire, how they started could not be explained. To make the incident even more notable, it was reported in the newspaper as being the first time an insurance company had paid out on a claim for damage caused by a ghost.

With activity ongoing, the property was investigated by The Society for Psychical Research and world-renowned investigator and author, Harry Price, but an answer as to what was causing the activity could not be found. A bishop attended to carry out an exorcism, yet while he sat beside the fireplace to prepare, his hat levitated from his lap, and was thrown into the fire. The building was requisitioned and used to house Polish troops during the war years, and it is believed that an article titled 'No Rest at the Mansion' published in the American Weekly in July 1942, relates to the happenings experienced by the troops at Pitmilly, although the house is not directly named. To add to the ghostly happenings, Captain Jeffrey died in 1941, yet seemingly did not leave as his ghost was later seen in the house.

In 1947, with the house in new ownership, there were attempts to convert it into a luxury hotel, but the press once again turned their attention to the house and published the stories of the poltergeist activity. With the unexplained occurrences ongoing and guests becoming worried about their stay, the hotel ceased trading in 1967, after which the building was demolished. What triggered or was behind the paranormal activity at Pitmilly was never revealed, and with the house gone, the activity and history of the house was slowly forgotten. All that remains today is the stable blocks and stores.

The Green Lady of Fernie

Fernie Castle dates back to the 14th century, when the tower house was built for the MacDuff's, the Earls of Fife. In the 15th century, ownership was passed to the Fernie family, and then several other wealthy owners, each altering and adding to the property, resulting in the building as it stands today, which operates as a hotel.

Fernie Castle

The castle is reported to be haunted by a green lady who is seen in a bedroom in the west tower. Green ladies are often associated with sadness, and the tale around the haunting certainly falls into this category. It is said that centuries ago, a local lady was fleeing her enraged father, who had discovered she was intending to marry a man he did not approve of. She hid in the room in the tower, but was found by her father. In the struggle that followed, she fell down the stairs to her death. Many suspect that she was in fact thrown down the steps by her father.

A number of unexplained incidents are reported to happen in the rooms in the tower, including electrical failures with batteries draining and power sources being turned off by unseen hands. One report claimed that every light in the tower was switched off simultaneously at the individual switches. For a few, the lonely figure of the Green Lady appears, with those who have witnessed the apparition saying she stands and stares with a mournful expression, before slowly vanishing.

The Headless Horseman of Stonehaven

On the ridge of a remote hilltop close to Stonehaven, there are 2 standing stones which are just over 70m apart, and are said to mark significant spots of a decisive battle in Scottish History, The Battle of Mons Graupius around AD 83 (some reports suggest it was a year later}. Although the location of the battle is disputed, this hillside is one of those suggested. Details of the battle, other than the location, are relatively well documented, thanks to the writings of a Roman biographer who wrote about the campaigns of Argicola in England, Wales and Scotland.

Argicola had already taken control of the lands from the River Tay south, yet he wanted more and marched a massive army of around 20,000 legionnaires north. Scotland at that time was split into a number of small kingdoms, each with its own tribe of people. With the Roman threat getting ever closer, Calgacus, the chief of one of the Caledonian tribes, sought assistance from the other kingdoms and amassed an army of over 30,000 to meet the Romans. It is documented that the battle was fought at the ridge of a hill, yet the exact geography is vague, hence the location being so heavily argued amongst scholars and historians.

Calgacus gathered his soldiers on the hilltop, giving him not only the advantage of greater numbers, but also holding the high ground, forcing the Romans to fight uphill. What he had not been able to account for however, was the experience of the Romans as an organised and structured fighting force. With his army made up from different tribes with different methods, Calgacus could not rely on numbers alone, and after bombarding the Caledonians with arrows and stones, the Roman foot soldiers moved forward to engage in hand to hand combat. The Caledonian cavalry used war chariots, which proved to be useless in the rough terrain whereas the Roman cavalry easily outflanked the opposing forces. It was a decisive victory for the Romans, with an estimated 10,000 killed on the Caledonian side, against around 360 Romans. The remaining 20,000 Caledonians fled back to their separate kingdoms, and although it is not certain what happened to Calgacus, most believe he too escaped.

The Standing Stones at Ring Cairn, the possible site of the Headless Horseman

The tale of the stones however, tell a different story. It is said that Calgacus was beheaded as he rode his horse across the ridge, most likely by a Roman Cavalryman, yet bizarrely he managed to keep riding his horse for some distance before finally falling. One of the standing stones is said to mark the spot where his head fell, and the other where his body fell. It is claimed that a headless horseman can be seen riding between the stones on dark nights, and believed that this is the phantom of Calgacus, repeating his final journey as his life energy drained from him.

The White Lady of St Andrews

This well known phantom walks both the cathedral grounds and the cathedral wall, always heading towards a tower built into the wall. Reports of sightings date back centuries, with there being a well documented incident of a fisherman making his way from the harbour to the town, where he spotted a white gloved hand waving at him as though trying to attract his attention from a small opening in the tower. Fearing someone was stuck, he rushed to help, only to find his own hand passed straight through the gloved hand when he tried to grab it before it slowly vanished. After this, the superstitious fishermen were said to always quicken their pace as they approached the tower, and pass as hastily as they could.

It was events in the later half on the 19th century that really added to the story. The cathedral ruins were undergoing extensive renovations to make them safe for visiting public, when one of the stonemasons leant on a stone in the old tower, and it moved. Curious, he tested the stone and was able to remove it, revealing a hidden chamber behind. He ventured in and found that there were 12 coffins inside, one with the lid open and containing the well preserved body of a young woman dressed entirely in white, including gloves. He reported the discovery, and was instructed to seal the chamber and carry on with the restoration.

Although the identity of the woman remained a mystery, it seemed the body of the White Lady had at least been discovered, and the reason why her ghost was always seen walking towards the tower was explained. Although attempts were made to keep the bodies a secret, word soon spread, and between the 1850s and the end of the century, a small handful of others managed to gain permission to access the chamber.

Each time the chamber was entered, the position of the coffins and bodies were reported differently, indicating that there had been undocumented access with someone moving the contents for some reason. When it was opened for the final time, the bodies were all gone and the coffins had been smashed. Who entered the tomb to remove the bodies and where they went was as much of a mystery as the identity of the bodies and why they were placed in the tower had been.

The Haunted Tower of St Andrews Cathedral

The White Lady is still seen walking the walls today, and I have several eye witness accounts. I was also fortunate enough to gain permission to access this tiny chamber, which is secured with an iron gate, while doing research for a book. Although the bodies have long gone, this confined space still contains a lot of energy.

The Handless Girl of Rait Castle

This fortified manor house in Nairn, near Inverness, is known to date back to 1165 when it was occupied by Shawn MacKintosh, son of Duncan MacDuff, the Earl of Fife. The castle passed through successive generations until 1274, when the last member of the family died with no heir of age to take on the castle. Instead, ownership was passed to the Cumming family who were part of the wider Comyn family of Castle Grant. As Norman Knights, the family also used the name 'De Rait', which is where the castle name originates. During the 14th century, the Cummings set about constructing much of the building that remains today, substantially rebuilding and extending the original property. The fortifications were also improved, with the new walls being 3m thick and surrounded by a defensive ditch.

This move to vastly improve the defences is perhaps a result of the family opposing the uprising of William Wallace and King Robert the Bruce, which most certainly would have placed them in great danger. Throughout this time, the MacKintosh family sought to use their opposition to the popular leaders of the country to try to reclaim the castle for themselves, and a feud followed.

In an attempt to resolve the dispute, the Cumming's invited the heads of the Mackintosh family to the castle to discuss the matter. But it was a trap. A plan was in place that the Mackintosh's would be asked to give up their weapons as they entered the castle, and during the meal when the traditional toast to the dead was given, that would be the signal for the Cumming's to draw their swords and slaughter the Mackintosh family. Unknown to the Clan Chief of the Cumming family, one of his daughters was in love with one of the sons of the Cumming family, and they had been seeing each other throughout the feud. She told her lover of the plans, and the Mackintosh men arrived with concealed weapons.

All was seemingly going to plan. The Mackintosh's had willingly given up the weapons that they carried as they entered, and this avoided any suspicions being raised. The meal had gone well, and as the Clan Chief started the toast to the dead, the sound of the Cumming's drawing their swords filled the hall. The Mackintosh's leapt to their feet, armed with Dirks (small traditional Scottish knifes) that they had hidden in their socks, and before the Cumming's knew what was happening, they were attacked and killed. The Clan Chief fled the scene and ran up the main tower of the castle in an attempt to find a place to hide, and it was there that he found his daughter trying to escape from the window. As she pleaded for forgiveness, he realised it was her who had revealed their plans of the ambush, and in a fit of rage he swung his sword at his daughter, cutting off both of her hands as she jumped from the window. Unable to break her fall, the impact with the ground was fatal.

After the massacre, the castle was occupied by various families for short periods of time, but never again as a permanent residence, and it soon fell into disrepair. Claims that the ghostly figure of a young lady with no hands waking through the castle and in the surrounding have been made since the time of the massacre, and this may be the reason for no-one staying there for long, and the castle eventually being abandoned.

Lady Crawford of Springfield

This ghost story comes from one of the most unusual properties in Scotland, Crawford Priory. Originally a modest lodge built for the Earl of Crawford in 1758 for use when he was visiting the area, it was when the estate was passed to his sister, Lady Mary Crawford, that the building was transformed into one of the most impressive Gothic mansions in the country.

The grand entrance to Crawford Priory

Lady Crawford had no family and lived her life as somewhat of a recluse, yet as part of the estate she inherited farms and coal mines, bringing her vast wealth. She seems to have chosen the lodge on the estate as the focus of her attention, possibly due to the remote location, and work began in 1809. No expense was spared, with extensive use of marble, hand printed wallpaper ordered from London, and extensive stable blocks for her beloved horses. The resulting mansion included 32 heated rooms, servants' quarters, and a great hall. Preferring the company of animals to humans, Lady Crawford continued to live a life of solitude, surrounded by animals she brought into the estate. When she died in 1833, Lady Crawford's funeral was held in the great hall, before her body was laid to rest in the family mausoleum on the hill overlooking the Priory.

The spirit of Lady Crawford is still reported to be seen wandering the grounds around her old home, with many people who have witnessed her sensing that she is still tending to her animals, who are also in spirit. A feeling of being watched in certain parts of the building are common, and Lady Crawford's ghost has been reported being seen at the roadside close to her mausoleum and even walking through former agricultural buildings which have since been converted to housing. With her former home now sadly being a ruin, it can only be hoped that it still appears to her as it did during her life and that she cannot see the fate that befell her mansion.

The Grey Lady of Burleigh Castle

Burleigh castle, which sits just outside the village of Milnathort, is unusual in design as it consists of both a square tower house, and a circular tower house connected by a central building.

The square tower house is in fact all that remains of an earlier castle that stood on the site, constructed in the 15th century for Sir John Balfour, and his wife Margaret. By the 16th century, the castle was in the ownership of Sir James Balfour, who extended the castle to add the central building and the circular tower. It is believed this was in fact part of a defensive wall that would have enclosed the castle, with a circular tower on each corner, although only one survives today.

The towers of Burleigh Castle

In 1707, the family's fortunes started to decline when Robert, the son of the 4th Lord Balfour, was accused of murdering a local schoolteacher. It is said that Balfour had fallen in love with a local woman, which did not meet the approval of his family, and so they sent him abroad in the hope the time away would make him forget her. It didn't work, and when he returned he hoped to rekindle their relationship, but found that she was already married to a school teacher. In a fit of rage, he killed him, after which he was detained awaiting trial. He somehow managed to escape, and is believed to have hidden inside a hollow tree in the castle grounds for several days, before fleeing abroad.

Robert Balfour returned to Scotland after his father's death, and aided the 1715 Jacobite uprising against the Royalists. Following the defeat of the Jacobite forces, the government seized the land belonging to all those who had supported them, including Burleigh Castle. The castle later passed through several other families, but was never again used as a home, and it soon fell into a state of disrepair.

The castle is said to be haunted by a grey lady who is seen walking through the grounds of the former courtyard. The ghost is locally known as 'Grey Maggie', linking her to Margaret Balfour, the wife of Sir John Balfour. Others also report a feeling of being watched while in the castle grounds, and it is believed this may be the ghost of Robert Balfour, condemned to forever remain within the hollowed tree in which he hid.

The Witch of Abergeldie

Abergeldie castle sits on the banks of the River Dee, just a few miles from the famous Royal holiday home, Balmoral Castle. Built around 1550 as a tower house for Sir Alexander Gordon, the castle remains in the ownership of the Gordon family today, and has seen an unusually large number of distinguished guests stay there due to being leased to the Royal Family for many years to house guests visiting Balmoral.

Abergeldie Castle taken from the summit of Creag nam Ban

At the end of the 16th century, a French woman named Katie (also known as Kittie) Rankin was employed at the castle as a servant. She worked happily there for many years yet Katie was an observant young woman, and definitely too vocal for her own good in these difficult times. According to local legend, she had witnessed the Laird leave the castle on unplanned journeys several times and, curious as to where he was going, learned that he was visiting his mistress. One fateful day the Laird's wife noticed he was missing and asked Katie if she had seen him, to which she replied that he was with his mistress at a nearby property.

The Laird's wife was enraged at learning that her husband may be having an affair, yet rather than direct her anger towards him, poor Katie faced her wrath. She accused Katie of being a witch and having second sight, which had allowed her to see her husband with his mistress and ordered that she be held in a small pit prison beneath the main tower of the castle. She is reported to have spent many days, possibly even weeks, chained to the walls of the dark, damp cell until she faced trial and was inevitably found guilty of witchcraft. In 1603, she was taken to a high point on the hillside close to the castle, where she was chained to a wooden stake upon a pile of wood, and burned alive. A cairn marks the approximate location where she faced the flames on the hill, which is now known as Creag nam Ban, meaning Hill of the Women, or the Witch.

A more elaborate version of the tale tells that Katie was known to have second sight by the Laird's wife, and while he was travelling abroad, she had asked Katie if she could see where he was. Katie did as she was asked, and reluctantly told her that her husband was in the arms of another woman. Enraged, the wife asked Katie to muster a storm and sink his ship. Katie explained she could not do that, but as fate would have it, while travelling home, the Laird's ship was sunk in a storm. No doubt regretting her actions, his wife accused Katie of witchcraft, and her fate was sealed.

Hill walkers have claimed to have caught a glimpse of a young woman wearing very old fashioned clothing who vanishes as they try to get a better look. Many believe this is the phantom of Katie returning to the spot where he she met her agonising death. Her figure is also seen walking within the castle, mainly in the prison area where she spent so much time suffering while awaiting her trial. When the wind is strong, locals report hearing Katie's screams coming from the hill where she perished.

As a side note, the castle was almost completely destroyed in 2015 when severe flooding of the River Dee washed away the road and much of the surrounding land, leaving it just feet from collapsing into the river. Fortunately, swift action to strengthen the bank saved it.

The Secretive Ghost of Rossend Castle

The castle can trace its origins back to around 1119, when a tower house known as The Tower of Kinghorne Wester, is known to have stood on the site. Over the years the tower-house was extended and became known as Abbot's Hall, and is likely to have been used as a residence for the Abbot of nearby Dunfermline Abbey, which controlled the surrounding land.

Between 1552 and 1554, the castle was extensively remodelled, with the original keep tower being rebuilt, and only the ground floor of the original 1119 being retained.

Rossend Castle

Over the centuries, further additions and alterations were made, with the last private owner being James Shepherd, who owned one of Kirkcaldy's many linoleum factories. When he died in 1907, the castle was bought by the local town council to give them the rights to the land in front to extend the docks and to build houses in the grounds leaving the castle today in the unusual location of being within a housing estate.

In 1972, the castle was in such poor condition that it was to be demolished, but was saved by a local architects firm, who restored it and used it as their offices.

It was during this time that reports of incidents begun, which were later passed onto myself. These included a general feeling of discomfort around the central staircase, with some always running on the stairs after dark to minimise the time they were there. There were also claims of footsteps being heard on the stairs and in the Great Hall, which was used as the main office area. Shadow figures were also seen, but only ever a fleeting glance before they vanished out of sight.

Curious about the reports, I carried out my own research on the castle and believe I may have found the identity of the ghost. In 1563 Mary, Queen of Scots, stayed overnight at the castle while travelling to St. Andrews. Among those travelling with her was Pierre de Chastelard, a young French nobleman who the Queen had become fond of for the poetry he wrote during her time in France. On that fateful night, having retired to her bed chamber with her maids, the Queen let out a loud scream, which brought her guards rushing into the room. Chastelard was found to be hiding under the Queen's bed, stating he was waiting to spend time alone with her. It transpired a similar incident had occurred in Edinburgh, just a few weeks earlier, for which the Queen had forgiven Chastelard, but this time he was not so lucky. She had wanted him killed on the spot, but was advised to make a public exhibition of him.

A week later, in front of a large crowd in St Andrews and the watchful eye of the Queen, he was beheaded. Just before his execution, he looked towards the queen and shouted, "Adieu, loveliest and most cruel of princesses", showing his love for the Queen remained.

With the last place that Chastelard had pursued his love interest with the Queen being Rossend Castle, it is entirely possible that he remains there today, still looking for the love of his life, and continuing to hide in the shadows as he had pursued her in life.

The Curse of Alloa Tower

Constructed in the late 14th century for the Erskine family, the future guardians of the Stuart Monarch heirs, Alloa tower was intended to provide protection for their boats on the River Forth. The family gained the title of the Earl of Mar, and in the 17th century, the 6th Earl carried out extensive remodelling on the interior of the tower, including a spectacular staircase and new entrance. By this time, a mansion house had also been added to the tower, however in 1800 this was destroyed by fire. The tower survived due to its thick, stone walls. The mansion was rebuilt, with work being completed in 1838.

Alloa Tower

After being in the ownership of the Erskine family for generations, it was lost to them and later abandoned, quickly falling into a state of disrepair. By the mid 1900s, the mansion house required to be demolished due to its poor condition, and the tower was only saved thanks to the Local Authority stepping in to provide a restoration fund. The National Trust for Scotland now own the building.

It would be easy to put the property being abandoned down to the running costs, but there may be a more sinister reason. The tower was believed to be cursed. Some say the curse was placed on the building by Thomas the Rhymer, who is famed for his ability to predict the future, and placing curses on those who wronged him. A more probable culprit was, however, the Abbot of Cambuskenneth Abbey. The 12th century abbey sits close to the tower, and was extensively damaged during the Reformation, with the last monks leaving in 1560. In 1562, John Erskine acquired the abbey remains and used the stone to build himself a house in Stirling, which infuriated the homeless Abbot.

As far as curses go, this one is pretty in-depth and included a number of elements. It was said that the Earl's position would be raised until he sits in the place of the King, but his work would never be finished, 3 of his children would never see the light of day, and that his land and titles would be taken from him and given to a stranger. It is clear someone was really upset with him. It was also said that the curse would be lifted when horses were stabled in the tower, a weaver had carried out his work in the Earl's chamber, and an ash sapling grew from the highest point of the tower.

The first part of the curse came true when the Earl became Guardian to the Stuart Monarch heirs, including helping the infant Mary, Queen of Scots escape to France and later supervising her son James VI. The position of Guardian was used when the King or Queen were too young to rule, and so the Guardian acted on their behalf, effectively meaning the Earl was sitting in the place of the King.

There is, however, another more sinister belief as to how this part of the curse was fulfilled. When Queen Mary stayed at Alloa Tower with her young son James, it was believed that he died, yet the Queen later continued her travels with her son by her side. The rumours started that, knowing the death of James would plunge the country into chaos, the Earl had allowed Mary to secretly take his own son, who was around the same age, in his place. If true, this would have resulted in the future Earl instead being raised as the future King, and taking the place of James.

Work on the Earl's new home, Mar's Wark in Stirling, which was being built with the stone from the Abbey, was constantly hindered and eventually had to stop. It had been completed to a standard where it could be lived in, and ironically King James VI stayed here when he was an adult. The property was however never fully completed, and many believe this satisfied the part of the curse saying that the Earl's work would never be completed.

Mar's Wark, Stirling

Three of the children born into the Erskine Family are said to have been born blind, meaning they would never see the light of day. The final part of the curse came true when the Erskine family were stripped of their land and titles for their support of the Jacobites, and they were sold to a distant member of the extended of the family. The curse was fulfilled, but remained in place, and so it is understandable that it could have been an oppressive place to live.

After the property fell into a state of disrepair, the Scot's Dragoons were believed to have taken ownership of the building and stabled their horses on the ground floor. Later, after being evicted from his premises in town, a local weaver is said to have moved his work to the abandoned tower, choosing the Earl's former chamber as a weaving room. Several ash saplings are noted to have been removed from the top of the tower during essential repair work in the early 19th century and, with the requirements to lift the curse now being completed, it seems luck once again befell the Erskine's, with them being restored to the position of the Earls of Mar in 1824.

Despite the curse being lifted, the tower is still believed to hold dark energy. Many visitors report feeling uneasy while touring, sometimes needing to leave the building, with the fireplace in the Great Hall making people feel so uncomfortable they refuse to go near it. The spirit of a serving girl is reported to be seen within the tower, and although not documented, it is possible that her death is in some way associated with this fireplace. A painting, known as the Lady in Black, is said to mist over and both staff and visitors report numerous cold spots throughout the tower, with visitors also reporting feeling a cold hand touch them.

A monk in black robes is seen in and around the tower, which may add to the rumours that the Earl of Mar did not only use that stone from Cambuskenneth Abbey, but was also responsible for putting together the mob that attacked and destroyed the Abbey in the first place. A phantom prisoner is seen in the tower basement, and on the anniversary of the mansion house being destroyed by fire, the tower is said to fill with the smell of smoke.

One further ghost, which raises questions, is that of a young child. With reports that an infant's skeleton was found in the tower during renovation, this adds to the story that the future King James VI died while staying there with his mother, and that his ghost still wanders through the building looking for her. That, sadly, is a mystery that will never be answered.

The Shadow-Man of Newark Castle

Standing in a cliff-top position just outside the village of St Monans, Fife, a castle is believed to have occupied this site since the 13th century.

The original castle was constructed on behalf of Sir Alan Durward, an important political figure of the 13th century, who was also credited with funding the construction of the shrine to St Monan, which King David attended and recovered from his injuries.

In 1649, the castle was purchased by a notable figure in Scottish History, David Leslie. Leslie was an accomplished military commander who had played a significant role in the Scottish Civil Wars, which started in 1640. In 1651, his army faced Oliver Cromwell's forces at the Battle of Worcester, where he was massively outnumbered and defeated.

Leslie was held prisoner in the Tower of London until Charles II was restored to the throne in 1660 when he was released. His lands and property had been taken from him following his imprisonment in 1651, however, with a large sum of money granted to him by the King in recognition of his military achievements, he returned to Scotland and once again purchased the castle and estate. The King also bestowed the title of 1st Lord of Newark to Leslie, and he set about extensively extending and remodelling the castle.

The remains of Newark Castle

Newark is long believed to have connections to smuggling over the centuries, with tales of secret tunnels and passageways leading down to the beach beneath, and also to St Monans Church. A shadowy figure has been reported on many occasions lurking within the ruins of the castle, and there is some debate as to who this is. Many believe it to be one of the smugglers, remaining to protect his ill-gotten goods that may still remain in hidden chambers below the castle, while others suggest it is David Leslie, returning to the castle he sacrificed so much to own. With talk of a tunnel linking the castle to the church, there are some who believe the phantom at St Monans church is not in fact a woman, as widely reported, but David Leslie in his fineries, including a wig.

The Curious Case of St Monans Church

The church of St Monans is unusual in that it is 'T' shaped, rather than the traditional cruciform. The church is also reported to be the closest church to the sea in the country, with the boundary wall of the churchyard doubling up as the sea wall. There are conflicting stories on the origins of the church, but some say St Monan himself visited during the 7th century and had a chapel built on the site, while others say his relics were brought here in the 9th century, and a shrine was built to house them.

St Monans Church

The site was believed to have magical healing powers. This reputation grew in the 14th century, when it is claimed that King David II, son of Robert the Bruce, was brought here having suffered severe injuries at battle.

Miraculously, he made a full recovery, and to show his appreciation to the Saint, he funded the construction of a new, larger church on the site. Work started in 1362, and took 8 years to complete. The church was extensively damaged by attacking English naval forces in 1544, during the period in history known as 'the rough wooing', when King Henry the 8th of England was trying to force a marriage between his son, Edward, and the young Mary, Queen of Scots.

The church later became connected with the witch trials in Scotland. One of the main methods to break those accused into confessing to witchcraft was sleep deprivation, and it may be from an incident at St Monans where this tradition was strengthened.

In the 15th Century, a local woman named Grizzie was accused of witchcraft, and sentenced to be burned at the stake. While waiting to be taken to be executed, the guards thought nothing of her falling asleep. They had already done their job and had the confession. As soon as she fell into a deep sleep, however, it is said she transformed into a droning beetle and escaped. She was never again seen in human form, and all those who were involved in her trial and conviction were plagued for the rest of their lives with the sound of a droning beetle in their ears. After this, no witch was to be allowed to sleep, even after conviction. For the witches that were burnt at the stake, their ashes were placed in a loft space in the top of the church steeple known as the Brunt Laft, where the wind from the sea would blow and scatter them far and wide.

The church is said to be haunted by the figure of a woman. In one reported incident, a young man whose role it was to clear and relight the furnace in the church had just completed his duties and was leaving the church, when his eye was drawn to a light shining from high up in the spire. He was mesmerised by the light on such a dark morning, and as he watched, he was suddenly gripped with fear when he realised it had developed into the face of a woman who was looking back at him.

He fled to the minister's house and, as he was recalling what he had just witnessed, he fell silent. Behind where the minister stood was a painting of his deceased wife, and the young man instantly recognised her as the face that he had seen at the tower moments earlier. Off course with the connection of the witch trials to the church tower, many believe instead that the ghostly woman is in fact one of those accused of witchcraft, and left in the tower to be scattered by the wind rather than given a Christian burial.

The Green Lady of Ashintully

Situated in a remote location, close to the small village of Carmichael, Ashintully castle was built as a fortified tower house for Colonel David Spalding in 1583. The Spalding family were long standing supporters of the Scottish Monarchy, and Colonel David took his forces to fight for the King of Spain in the 8 year battle for Flanders. It was plunder brought back from Flanders that he used to build the castle, which was based on the nearby Whitefield Castle, a hunting lodge built for King Malcolm III in 1060.

Ashintully Castle, which now appears more a manor house after several alterations carried out over the centuries

His son, Andrew Spalding, became head of the Clan upon the death of Colonel David and was the first Spalding to occupy the castle long term. It seems however that, for an unknown reason, he was deeply unpopular to the extent that in 1587, a group put together by his neighbours, kidnapped and held him prisoner. After being subjected to torture, he was eventually released and sought the help of the King, who declared his captors to be rebels. The loyalty to the monarchy ceased with the next generation of the Spalding Family with his successor, David, being involved in the Gowrie Conspiracy, an incident shrouded with mystery that was most likely a failed attempt to kidnap King James VI. The Castle later provided refuge for the famous outlaw, Rob Roy MacGregor, and for the Jacobite leaders. In the 19th century, the castle passed into the ownership of the Aytoun family, with successive generations staying there until 1948, when it was again sold. Today the castle remains a family home, with the estate offering high-class accommodation and outside sporting facilities.

The best-known castle ghost is that of Green Jean. The tale behind the phantom is one of murder and vengeance. It is said that Jean was a senior family member who was quite a dominant woman and liked to get her own way. Knowing that in these superstitious times, green was seen as a faerie colour and not one for humans to wear, she had made her intentions clear one evening that she would be wearing a green dress to dinner regardless of her family's objections. Her uncle, seemingly fed up with her previous actions, decided to take matters into his own hands, and went to her bedroom where he found her maid still attending to her hair. He killed the maid to ensure there were no witnesses, and then cut his nieces throat. Rather unceremoniously, he had the maid's body hidden in the chimney, while his niece's body was taken to the family burial ground. Any hope that she would be laid to rest there were however dashed, when her mournful figure began to be seen walking within the castle and the burial ground, seeking revenge for her murder.

Green Jean is not the only vengeful spirit. A ghost known as Crooked Davie is also said be seeking retribution. Davie is reported to have been a hunchback, but well known for being a great runner, and so he was employed at the castle as a messenger. On the day of a banquet, Davie was sent to deliver an urgent message. He did not want to go, as he knew not only would all the staff eat well that night from the leftover food from the banquet, but he had also started to date one of the maids and planned to meet up with her. He set out, running as fast as he could to deliver the message, and returned with the reply just before the banquet ended. He waited in the hallway for the banquet to finish so he could deliver the response, but exhausted, he fell asleep in front of the fire. When his master found him, he could not believe that he had already delivered the message, and no doubt in a drunken rage at being disobeyed, he drew his sword and killed Davie where he lay. It was not until he took the papers from his pocket, that he realised it was in fact the reply.

Davie's phantom has been seen walking within the castle and the grounds ever since, along with the third ghost of the castle, a tinker who was executed for trespassing after being found on the property. It is said that he was hung from a tree on the long drive to the castle, and as the noose was being placed around his neck, he uttered a curse that the Spalding family line at Ashintully would soon end. The curse came true, and it was not long after this that ownership passed to the Aytoun family, yet the tinker is still seen walking along side Crooked Davie, still shouting his curse to anyone who will listen.

The Phantom Monk of Balmerino

The church within the abbey at Balmerino was founded in 1226, although building work on the site carried on for many years after. It was established as a Cistercian Abbey by the monks at Melrose Abbey in the Scottish Borders and housed up to twenty monks.

Balmerino Abbey

In 1547, the Abbey was attacked by invading English forces and extensively damaged. It was repaired, but suffered far worse damage in the reformation when followers of John Knox destroyed the abbey, killing all of the monks that remained.

Following the creation of the peerage, with the title 'Lord of Balmerino', the remains of the abbey and its grounds formed part of the geographical barony of the first Lord of

Balmerino, James Elphinstone, in 1604. Today the Abbey remains in a ruinous condition with the church building fenced off due to its dangerous condition.

The ghosts of the murdered monks are said to still roam the grounds with many reports of their spectral figures being witnessed pushing wheelbarrows as though continuing with their day-to-day chores. Another spirit which is said to haunt the abbey is reported to be seen sitting in the cellars, and is thought to be a monk who was responsible for keeping a watch on the corn stored in the cellars to ensure rats and mice did not eat it.

The Giant Piper of Cortachy Castle

The history of the Ogilvy family can be traced back for hundreds of years. In the 11th century, the Earl of Gilchrist was charged with the murder of his wife, and his sons were also charged with being involved in the murder of their mother. Being of noble stock, they all were spared execution, but were stripped of their lands and titles. Not long after, King William the Lion was travelling through the Glen of Ogilvy, when he was attacked. By chance, the former Earl was in the area and came to the rescue of the king, fighting off the robbers. Upon learning who his defender was, the King issued a full forgiveness to the Earl, restored his land and titles, and added the Glen of Ogilvy to his estates. The glen was later passed to the Earl of Gilchrist's brother, Gilbert, who assumed the title the Earl of Ogilvy, after his land.

Cortachy Castle

With the successive Earls of Ogilvy becoming the heir to the lands of the Airlie Family, Earls of Findlater and Seafield and the Barons of Banff, the family grew to become one of the most important in the country. On 28th April 1491, the 9th Earl, James Ogilvy, was knighted to become Sir Ogilvy, and acquired the lands of all of the abbeys and Baronies in the surrounding counties.

Marion Ogilvy, the daughter of Sir James Ogilvy, was the lover of Cardinal Beaton of St Andrews. By pure fortune, she was leaving the castle just as a group of men were entering on the morning of 29th May 1546. These men were the supporters of George Wishart, and went on to lay siege to the castle and murder the Cardinal. This was not the only connection to St Andrews Castle that the Ogilvy family had. As devout Royalists, the family received many favours from the monarchy for successive generations.

The family fought for the Royal forces against the Covenanters, and in 1646, after a Royalist defeat at battle, James Ogilvy was taken prisoner and held at St Andrews Castle. Having been sentenced to be beheaded, his sister sought permission to visit him before he was executed. The request was granted and she arrived at the castle on the evening of the 19th January 1646, dressed in her finest clothing. Unknown to all, this was part of a plan to break James out of prison. After being allowed in to meet him, she persuaded him to swap clothes with her. James then simply walked out of the castle disguised in the heavy female clothing and aided by the darkness of the evening. When his sister was discovered, rather than be charged, she too was set free.

The loyalty of the family to the Royals was to be their downfall. They fought for the Stuart Monarchy during the Jacobite rebellions, and after the Jacobite defeat at Culloden, the Ogilvies lost much of their land and most titles. David Ogilvy escaped to France, where he became a General in the French Kings service. By 1896, the titles had been largely restored to the family.

The ghost story comes from Cortachy Castle. Originally built for the Earls of Strathearn in the 15th century, this fortified mansion house was acquired by the Ogilvy family in 1473. As is so often the case, the origin of the ghost story is shrouded with mystery. Some say that a drummer at the castle simply fell foul of the Lady of the castle. Other versions tell that the drummer fell in love with the Lady, incurring the wrath of the Lord, or that he had carried a message to the castle from a much hated enemy Lord, or that he had failed to warn the occupants of the castle of an advancing enemy army. Whatever the unfortunate drummer had done, he was sewn inside his own drum. He is said to have begged for his life to be spared throughout the process, and when it became clear his pleas were being ignored, he vowed to haunt the castle forever. The drum, with the drummer inside, were taken to the top of the castle and thrown down onto the rocks below.

The phantom drummer is said to be at least 9 feet tall, and is sometimes accompanied by ghostly pipers when he appears. His sighting is said to signify the passing of a senior member of the family approaching, and there are at least 2 noted cases where he was seen just before a death, the most recent being in 1900 when he was seen and heard just before the Earl died in the Boer War. This was the last time he has appeared, perhaps after centuries of haunting, the spirit of the drummer finally deciding it was time to rest in peace.

The Whistling Wraith of Balcomie Castle

Like many other Scottish castles, Balcomie was originally constructed as a tower house. Built in the early 16th century, the six-storey stone building may well stand on the site on an earlier building. Little seems to be known about the building's exact history, however it is known that several noble families owned it and a large extension was added to form a mansion house, most likely towards the end of the 16th century. The castle eventually became the property of the Earl of Kellie who had the newer wing substantially dismantled, possibly to allow the stone to be re-used at the nearby Kellie Castle and its walled gardens, leaving only the original tower intact.

The castle was left in a state of disrepair until the early 19th century when additional buildings were built on the site of the former mansion house to create a farmhouse, offices, and farm buildings. The property is still operated as a farm, and although the tower house is not occupied, the 19th century additions can be rented as holiday accommodation.

There are a number of claims of strange happenings at the castle such as items of furniture being moved around and candles burning blue. The spirit of a boy/young man has also been witnessed at the castle on many occasions, both inside and up on the battlements of the castle. He is said to have been a servant at the castle with a very jovial personality, which led him to whistle almost constantly both while he worked and during rest periods.

The tower of Balcomie Castle

Eventually the castle owner at the time got so frustrated at the constant sound of whistling that he locked the boy in the dungeon as a punishment. Unfortunately, it seems the boy was then forgotten about until around a week later, when he was found dead from starvation and lack of water. Whistling is said to have been heard from the vaulted area in which the boy was held, and the figure is often said to be holding or playing an old tin whistle.

The Sad Tale of Castle Grant

Castle Grant sits in a remote spot near Granton-on-Spey in the Highlands of Scotland. Originally known as Freuchie Castle, the tower house of the Grant dates back to the 16th century and was built for the Comyn family. In 1694, the castle was passed to the Grant family. It was renamed to reflect this, and it became the seat of the Clan Grant chiefs of Strathspey.

Castle Grant

The castle is said to be haunted by Lady Barbara Grant, one of the daughters of an early clan chief. She is thought to have fallen in love with a local man, yet as he was of a lower class, her father forbid the romance. Instead, he found a man for her to marry who he deemed to be of a more suitable standing. Barbara rebelled and refused to marry her father's choice, so he decided to force her to change her mind. Within the tower, there is a tiny room with no windows, with the door hidden behind tapestries. This room was known to the castle occupants as 'the blackness' which gives an idea of how much it was feared. Barbara was locked in the room, with orders given that she was to be kept in there until she changed her mind and agreed to go through with the wedding.

It is not known how long she was held in The Blackness, or how much food and water was given to her, but she did die within that room. Legend tells it was from a broken heart, yet it was more likely to be from ill-health and malnutrition suffered while being kept in such cramped, unsanitary conditions. Ever since her ghostly figure has been seen walking through the tapestry that hides the door, pausing briefly to rub her hands together as though washing them, before turning and passing back through the tapestry to the concealed room. This is perhaps a sign that at least one of the servants in the castle had taken pity on her and, at great risk to themselves, had let her out of the room to wash herself when they could, and she still relives this act of kindness.

It is reported that the room was opened in the 1880s with some anticipation as to whether the remains of Barbara might still be within. No bones were found, leaving it unclear what happened to her body after her death. Instead, a number of swords and muskets were discovered showing it had been used as a storeroom for some time. In more recent times, while some restoration was being carried out in the tower, the workmen reported hearing the sound of footsteps walking across the floor above them, before the creak of a door opening then closing, followed by a woman crying with despair. They are said to have left and refused to continue work.

The castle is also home to 2 other ghosts, one being a housemaid who still walks through the castle, carrying out her daily tasks, and the other being a phantom piper witnessed within the grounds. It is believed the piper had fled from the Battle of Culloden to alert the family, who fought for both the Government forces and the Jacobite forces, of the Jacobite defeat, yet he never made it and was slain before reaching the castle doors. There is however another possibility, members of the Comyn family were talented musicians, and served as the hereditary pipers and fiddlers of the Laird of Grant, and so it is possible the piper is from the Comyn family, returning to their original family home where they served as a piper for the new laird.

The Tale of 'Bluidy Bruce'

In 1546, Sir William Bruce, a consultant for the Scottish Royal Family, had Earlshall Castle built near the village of Leuchars in Fife, and this fine castle can count Mary, Queen of Scots and King James the VI and I amongst the distinguished guests who have stayed there. The castle remained the home of the Bruce Family, including Andrew Bruce, the 7th Earl, until it was abandoned around the 19th century and quickly fell into a ruinous state.

Earlshall Castle

The castle was fortunately restored and is now a private family home, however, the prior residents do not appear to have left. The spirit of a young maid is reported as being seen around the castle, as though still carrying out her duties, yet it is the ghost of Andrew Bruce that is the dominant phantom. Andrew Bruce was a brutal persecutor of the Covenanters, earning him the nickname 'Bluidy Bruce'. The figure of a large built man is reported as being seen standing in Andrew's former bedchamber, but more frightening, visitors have reported hearing heavy footsteps hastily approaching while on one of the staircases, giving the impression that they are not welcome and are being chased from the building.

The Spectral Sailor of the Glenlee

Built at Port Glasgow in 1896, the Glenlee operated as bulk cargo carrier, and travelled around the world a total of 4 times, a considerable feat during these dangerous times. In 1922, it was purchased by the Spanish Navy who used it for training until 1981, when it was de-rigged with plans to convert it to a museum. Instead, it was left exposed to the elements, unmaintained, in the port of Seville. By luck, as preparations were being made to scrap the ship in 1990, it was spotted by Naval Architect Sir John Brown who, after realising the significance of the Glenlee, started the wheels in motion that would ultimately see it back on the Clyde, fully restored, and operating as a tourist attraction. The boat is part of the core collection of the National Historic Fleet, being of outstanding national significance in terms of maritime heritage, historic associations, or technical innovation.

The Glenlee Tall Ship

Strange happenings were first reported on board by the contractors responsible for the restoration work with unexplained noises, shadow figures and tools going missing, only to reappear later exactly where they had been left. Staff members working on the boat have described similar noises and fleeting glimpses of figures, as have many visitors to the boat. One staff member tells that while she was doing a tour, the door handle on the door she was standing beside began to turn and rattle. Assuming someone had become separated from the tour group, she opened the door to find no-one was there. This incident was witnessed by all on the tour.

But who haunts the Glenlee, and why? As with all ships of the time, any sailor that died on the boat during a voyage would be buried at sea. Without facilities that we take for granted today, it would be impossible to isolate the body and prevent any disease spreading, and so disposing of the body was the only safe thing to do. On the Glenlee, one sailor stands out from all of the others for his suffering on board the boat, which may explain why his spirit may remain attached to it.

On 28th March 1912, the ships records show William Pedvin reported to the ships doctor complaining of bowel pain. This was just 28 days into a voyage that was to last more than a year. He was treated by the doctor and considered fit enough to return to his duties on 6th April. It seems he did not seek further treatment until 10th February 1913, when he was reported to the ships doctor for being drunk on board. This perhaps was an indicator that he had been using alcohol to deal with the pain he was suffering. On 24th February, he was admitted to the medical quarters with severe stomach cramps, but refused treatment. He returned to work for short spells at a time between periods of rest, but by 25th July, he was unable to continue and once again admitted to the medical quarters. He was soon back to work, but only 3 days later, once again was too ill and was back in the medical quarters before being moved to a makeshift hospital room at the rear of the ship, set up specially to treat him away from the rest of the crew.

By the 7th September, the records show his health was improving yet, as before, it was only a temporary recovery. On 12th September he was reporting chest pains and his mind was noted to be wandering, and 2 days later, on 14th September 1913, he died aged 54. His body was sewn into a heavy canvas, and at 8am the following morning was lowered on a platform from the side of the boat into the sea. His 18 month ordeal was finally over, although it seems the long suffering has left at least some of his energy on the Glenlee, where he still roams today.

The Smothered Piper of St Andrews

A now long lost tunnel is documented to have been once accessible via a small, triangular opening in the sea cliffs at St Andrews. With many superstitions around the tunnel, few entered, but those who did estimated that the tunnel was around 120 feet long, before it opened out into a chamber, from which 2 further tunnels continued with a carved cross between them. No-one was known to have dared venture further until one New Year's Eve, when a bold young piper affectionately known as Jock, said he would see where the tunnels go.

The cliff where the entrance to the cave once was

Despite his wife begging him not to, Jock entered the tunnels, playing his pipes as he went to allow those above ground to follow the music to track his route. The small, but eager, gathered crowd followed the pipes to around the centre of the town, where they suddenly fell silent. Jock's wife waited for days at the tunnel entrance for her husband, but he never returned. With no-one being prepared to go in looking for him, Jock was lost.

The following New Years Eve, Jock's wife was seen walking to the tunnel entrance stating she was 'going to her Jock'. She too entered the tunnel and was never seen again.

Despite the tunnel entrance being lost many years ago due to coastal erosion, the ghost of Jock is still seen walking where the cliff has now collapsed, still playing his pipes. The spirit of his wife is also seen at Hogmanay, pacing where the tunnel entrance once lay. Locals fear hearing the sound of Jock's pipes echoing up from the cliffs, as to hear the pipes is considered a warning of a pending death in the family.

The Dark Monk of Fidra

Fidra is one of a cluster of 5 small islands in the Forth, with a long and sometimes dark history. The island formed part of the Barony of Dirleton, which was granted to John de Vaux by King David 1st during the 12th century. A chapel was situated on the island, which was dedicated to St Nicholas in 1165, and the de Vaux family had a castle built as a small stronghold, known as Tarbert Castle. Island living in the harsh environment of the Firth of Forth was to prove to not suit John de Vaux's successors, and in 1220 the island was gifted to the monks of Dryburgh Abbey by William de Vaux. The family later had Dirlerton Castle built on the mainland as a home.

Fidra Island

The chapel served several purposes over the centuries. It became a place of pilgrimage for nuns, and at the time of its dissolution in 1561, it housed 11 nuns. The chapel was also used as a quarantine point for sailors returning to Leith from long sea voyages. They would be dropped at the island to be nursed by the nuns, and allowed to be taken to land once they had recovered. It is not clear what happened to those who did not recover.

When the great plague of 1645 struck nearby Edinburgh, the chapel was one of several locations used as a hospital, again to quarantine the ill. Although it was described as a hospital, it is doubtful whether much care was given and the ill were most likely left to fend for themselves. The chapel may have returned to serve as a hospital for sick sailors after the plague, although with the nuns gone, there would be little assistance available to them. It was later believed to have been used to hold Jacobite soldiers, as was the notorious prison at the Bass Rock. Although it is not noted whether any Jacobite prisoners died on the island, it is known 40 perished at the Bass Rock, so it is likely that some of those held on Fidra also lost their lives.

The island was later believed to be the inspiration for the author Robert Louis Stevenson's novel 'Treasure Island', initially serialised in children's magazines before being released as a novel in 1883. In 1885 a lighthouse was built on the island, which is notable for the cable drawn railway line used to pull supplies up to the building due to the sheer drops around the edges of the island. An interesting fact noted as early as the 1400s is that the layout of the pyramids of Giza match the positions of 3 of the islands in the Forth, Fidra, the Lamb and Craigleith. The island is now uninhabited and is a controlled nature reserve.

With so much death on the island, it is not surprising it is haunted. The ghost story goes right back to the 12th century when the chapel was attacked by Vikings. Many of the religious settlements in and around the Firth of Forth suffered similar attacks, with the unarmed monks and nuns being slaughtered. The spirit, described as a large, hooded figure, is known as The Dark Monk of Fidra. Witnessed in and around the chapel ruins, little is known about the phantom other than he is said to have haunted the island for over 800 years, and successive generations have believed the island to be a place to be avoided because of the haunting. The name 'Fidra' is said to be Norse for Feather Island, or Island of the Feathers, further connecting it to the Vikings. It is unlikely to please the Dark Monk that the island he haunts carries a name from the language of his slayers.

The Mackie Poltergeist

At a farm named Ringcroft of Stocking, which sits close to the village of Auchencairn in Dumfries and Galloway, an incident in 1695 became known as one of the most remarkable episodes of demonology in the country. It started in February of that year when the farmer, Andrew Mackie, discovered that all of the ropes holding his cattle had been broken through the night. Considering it strange, he assumed something must have spooked them, and he purchased stronger ropes. To his dismay, the following morning he again found all had been broken. Fearing someone have been on the farm, the cattle were moved to an outbuilding, yet nothing could have prepared him for what was to follow.

As he approached the outbuilding he again saw the cattle were loose, their ropes broken, and the doors of the outbuilding open. Noises within the building drew his attention, and when he went to check, he found one of the cows was bound to a beam within the barn, its feet completely off the ground. This was a feat that would be physically impossible for a man to achieve, and one that would have been extremely difficult for even a group of men to do.

Needless to say, Andrew Mackie was concerned about what was happening and vowed to keep a close watch on the farm. That night, he was awoken by his wife's cries of panic. He suddenly became aware that the room was filled with smoke and found a pile of burning peat in the middle of the bedroom floor. Had his wife not woken up, they almost certainly would have perished in the fire, yet how the peat got there, and who set it alight was the real mystery.

The attacks on the family intensified in frequency, and by March, stones were being thrown at them by unseen hands on such a regular basis that many people witnessed this happening. Household items were going missing, only to reappear in completely random locations, and the children started to report being struck when no one was there. After 4 days of this, the family turned to the church for help.

Two days later, the Reverend Telfair visited the property to investigate the allegations. He looked around the house and outbuildings yet found nothing, but just as he was about to leave, he saw stones drop from the sky above the house, and heard the cries of the family inside. He went back into the house to find the family reporting that stones had again been thrown at them, and he decided it was best to say a prayer asking for divine intervention. As soon as he began, stones started to be thrown at him, but he persevered and completed the recital.

All seemed quiet for a short while before events started again, and the Reverend decided to return to stay the night. Throughout his stay, he was plagued by stones and other objects being thrown at him. He also reported feeling as though he was being struck hard, by what felt like an unseen staff, around his sides and shoulders. Although nothing could be seen, the 'swish' of the staff could be heard just before each strike. There were also multiple knocking noises coming from all around the room. Reverend Telfair had brought 2 witnesses with him, and they confirmed what happened that night. As he tried to pray, the Reverend reported seeing a white hand and arm from the elbow down grab his own arm and push down, as though trying to lower the prayer book.

Any hopes that the family had that the intervention of the church might help were immediately dashed. The activity in the house increased and became more violent. Even visitors to the farm began to be hit by flying stones and felt the strikes of the staff. Andrew Mackie had his hair pulled back so forcefully that his forehead was cut, and other family members were pulled across the house by their clothes. Items of furniture were reported to raise from the floor and move across the room before being dropped.

A short while later, Mrs Mackie found a small bundle of bones wrapped in what appeared to be skin beneath a loose step at the entrance of the house. Fearful of witchcraft, and with the family terrified and people refusing to go near the farm, the landlord, Charles Maclelland of Colline, stepped in and met with 2 ministers to report what had been happening. The ministers arranged to visit the house, and spent the night praying, yet as with others, they were constantly interrupted by stones being thrown at them. Some of the stones were found to weigh 7 pounds, and both suffered several injuries throughout the night. The family did not escape the spirits anger. They had lumps of flaming peat thrown at them, and when the sun rose, a shower of stones came down on all who remained in the house.

Realising that they needed help, the ministers arranged to return with the Reverend Telair and 3 other ministers. As soon as the Reverend began to pray, he was pounded with stones, before again they poured down from above on all present. Some of the ministers reported feeling hands grip their ankles and lift them from the floor, and several heard a gruff voice warn that if the land did not repent, it would summon more like it and would trouble every family in the country. The voice was also heard telling the churchmen to 'wheest'. Yet still the Reverend continued. In total the exorcism took 2 weeks, during which time the attacks continued a figure said to be made from cloth appeared. The disembodied voice reputedly said to have told them that it would continue to torment all until the following Tuesday. True to its word, on Tuesday 1st May, the activity ceased.

The family tried to return to normal, but with what had happened at the farm being well known, after a few months they moved out and the farm was abandoned. A ring of trees was planted around it, believed to be able to hold the evil within. A year after the incident, the Reverend Telfair published a report detailing the incidents along with witness testimonials, which is why so much detail is known.

Nothing remains of the farm today. The circle of trees became known as the Ghost Trees and only one remains, although it is dead and crooked. According to the legend that arose around the story, when the final tree falls, the Mackie Poltergeist will return to once again torment the area.

The Disaster at the Old Kirk

The Old Kirk in Kirkcaldy can be dated back to the 13th century. Despite common beliefs, it is relatively rare for a church or churchyard to be haunted, with most ghost stories associated around the location of a death or a location that played a significant part in someone's life, rather than the final resting place of their body. An incident on 15th June 1828, has however resulted in the Old Kirk reported to be very active with unexplained activity.

The Old Kirk, Kirkcaldy

On this day, the Reverend Edward Irving, a prominent clergyman who had strong connections with Kirkcaldy, was to deliver a sermon in the church. His presence attracted huge crowds resulting in the building being filled to capacity with more people standing outside. As the Reverend entered, the people in the gallery surged forward to catch a glimpse of him, and the sudden increase in weight at the front of the balcony caused it to collapse. In the tragedy, the falling beams killed two people, twenty-six people were trampled to death in the escaping crowds and approximately one hundred and fifty people were injured.

The ghost that has been reported from the Kirk appears to be a lone figure standing in the church, staring towards the corner where the balcony collapsed, as though still waiting for a loved one. A contractor also reports being pushed as he tried to climb a ladder in the area where the spirit is seen, possibly a warning not to go up high after what happened, and electrical items are reported to act odd, including switching on and off by themselves.

The Murdered Lord of Inchdrewer

Inchdrewer fortified tower house dates back to at least the 16th century. Originally built for and occupied by the Currour family, the castle has commanding views across the town of Banff and to the sea beyond. James Currour was a lawyer and notary in Banff, involved in writing contracts for the Ogilvies of Dunlugas who purchased the castle in 1557.

In the ownership of Walter Ogilvy, the castle was refurbished and extended to include a round tower and courtyard, and in 1633, King Charles 1st issued an Act to officially recognise the Ogilvies rights to the land and property. By this time, the castle was in the ownership of George Ogilvy, a devout Royalist who supported the King's campaign against the Covenanters. This resulted in the castle being attacked and largely destroyed by the Covenanter forces, led by General Robert Monro, in 1640. The castle was rebuilt, and in recognition of his loyalty, George Ogilvy was appointed as the First Lord Banff in 1642.

In 1713, the castle was once again devastated by fire, and in 1746 it was attacked by the Duke of Cumberland's forces during the Jacobite rebellion. In 1803, the 8th Lord Banff passed with no direct male heir, so ownership was passed to his sister, Jean, wife of George Abercrombie of Birkenhog. With the Abercrombie family having a main residence at Forglen House near Turriff, Inchdrewer Castle was surplus to requirement and was let out to various tenants until 1836, when it became unoccupied, and quickly fell into a state of disrepair.

Inchdrewer Castle

In 1963, the castle ruins were bought by Count Robin Mirrlees, who is considered to have been heavily influential in the characteristics of the fictional British agent, James Bond, through his work with Bond creator, Ian Fleming, while he was carrying out the research for the book 'On Her Majesty's Secret Service'. The castle was made wind and water tight, but was again abandoned. Upon Count Mirrlees death in 2013, the castle and the title of 'Baron of Inchdrewer' were put up for sale. The purchase by the current owners almost certainly saved the building, which was again exposed to the elements. It is again wind and water tight with restoration work ongoing.

The story of the haunting relates to the fire of 1713, when in the ownership of the 3rd Lord Banff, George Ogilvy who had inherited the estate upon the death of his father in September 1668. As a devout Roman Catholic, George Ogilvy caused some shock when he suddenly renounced his religious beliefs in 1705, and turned to the Protestant faith, yet there seems to have been a reason for this. He then supported an Act of Parliament to prevent the growth of the influence of the Pope, and in turn was allowed to take his seat in the Scottish Parliament. This was to be the final full Scottish Parliament, and in 1706 he gave his full support to the Act of the Union, which brought together the Scottish and English Parliaments to form the British Parliament. In return, he received a share of the £20,000 paid to the nobles who helped pass the Act, which came into effect in 1707.

This was a deeply unpopular act across Scotland and led to riots, leaving some nobles requiring protection. With tensions running high for decades after, this was perhaps what ultimately led to his death. Lord Banff spent a lot of time in Ireland, and in November 1713, when he returned to Inchdrewer from a trip there, he died in a mysterious fire. Although it was never proven, it was widely believed that his staff had ransacked the castle, stealing whatever they could. Upon his return, they had attacked and killed him before setting fire to the castle to hide their deed. This was seen by many as him receiving his judgement for his actions, and as late as the 1870s, over 150 years after his death, he was still being described as having sold his country and religion.

Ever since, his phantom is reported to have been seen within the castle. Described as looking particularly angry, it is thought he is still looking for the servants who murdered him in the hope to avenge his death. In the 1970s, the historical writer Nigel Tranter visited the castle and it is reported that as he approached, a large, white dog ran out from the castle towards him and the builder who accompanied him, before disappearing. The castle had been locked up for over a week, and with no explanation as to how the dog got in or out of the castle, or survived for a week with no water, this dog has been classed by many to be another ghost of the castle.

The Tragedy at Kellie Castle

Built in the 14th century, possibly on the site of an earlier castle, Kellie Castle originated as a tower house for the Oliphant family, who over the centuries added to the building.

Kellie Castle

In 1613, the castle was sold to Sir Thomas Erskine, the 1st Earl of Kellie, and remained the family home until 1797, when the 7th Earl died with no direct descendants, when the contents were sold and the building was passed to distant relatives, who did not stay there, and it fell into a state of disrepair.

In 1878, James Lorimer, the Professor of Law at Edinburgh University, took occupation of the castle, and an extensive restoration project commenced to bring the castle back to its former glory. Today the castle is owned by the National Trust for Scotland, although James Lorimer does not appear to have left the home in which he devoted so much time and expense to save.

Visitors to the castle report seeing a gentleman in period dress sitting in one of the chairs in a long corridor within the castle, and have later identified him from paintings as James Lorimer. A more curious ghost is that of Anne Erskine, who is said to have fallen to her death from a window in one of the stairwells. Her figure is rarely seen, yet there have been several reports of the sound of footsteps running on the stairs, and a pair of red shoes being witnessed rushing up the spiral staircase, which is believed to be Anne continuing to re-enact her final actions before she possibly tripped and fell.

The Phantom Vikings of Iona

Sitting off the west coast of Scotland, Iona has long religious connections. In the year 563, a young missionary monk named Columba, along with 12 followers, arrived at Iona from Ireland. They established a small settlement from which they actively set about converting Scotland to what became known as Celtic Christianity.

Columba's reach was far. He is documented to have travelled as far as Inverness where he met with the Pictish King Brude, and aided in converting him to the Christian faith. On his way to Inverness, Columba is said to have gone to the aid of some fishermen who had just lost one of their crew to a viscous water monster. Columba had one of his followers swim out into the Loch to attract the beast, and as it rose from the depths, ordered it to return to the darkness from which it had come and to never hurt anyone again. This is the first documented account of the now famous Loch Ness Monster.

Columba died in 597, just as Roman Christianity was arriving in England and began to spread north. The old Celtic ways remained strong in Scotland, however, in 802, Iona suffered a devastating attack from the Vikings. Further attacks followed, and over the next few decades the monks slowly moved from the island to the safety of the mainland. The centre of the Scottish Catholic Church moved from Iona to St Andrews, and the Roman ways were adopted.

View over the coast of Iona

Iona remained a sacred place and the burial place of the Kings. In a section of St Oran's Graveyard, the graves of some of the most famous and important names in Scottish history line is known as the Street of the Dead. Despite the island's history, the graveyard is also the burial place of many Viking kings. Although none of the original grave markers remain, an inventory taken in 1549 revealed that there were 48 Scottish Kings, 8 Norwegian Kings, and 4 Irish Kings buried there. These include King Kenneth MacAlpine, who is credited with uniting the Gaels and the Picts against their joint Viking enemy, creating the foundation for modern day Scotland, and King MacBeth, best known from Shakespeare's fictional play of the same name.

Iona Abbey dates back to around 1200, having been established to replace Columba's monastery by Reginald

MacDonald, son of Somerland, the King of the Isles, to maintain and build on the islands religious heritage. The importance of the Abbey grew and it was extended several times until the religious reformation of the 16th century saw the monks driven from it and the building ransacked. Today Iona remains a place of pilgrimage to thousands every year.

Many of the religious locations are reported to be haunted. Several figures are seen within the Abbey, often all at the same time, as though they still carrying out their duties. A picture taken in 1900 is said to show several of these phantoms.

The most unusual ghost story comes from an area known as Martyr's Beach where 68 monks were slain by invading Vikings in the year 806. Reports have been made of witnessing the slaughter, with ghostly Viking longships appearing just off the shore before the marauding Norsemen leap into the shallow water and charge forward towards a group of ghostly monks, attacking them where they stand. The Vikings are then said to disappear before returning a short while later carrying gold and leading cattle back towards their waiting ships as the sky above the Abbey turns red. Once all is loaded onboard, the ships simply vanish as they sail off.

The Cursed Necklace of Loch Leven

A story published in the Courier and Advertiser Newspaper on 1st November 1937 tells a strange tale of a necklace that had been sent to Scotland from Cairo. The identity of the person who sent it is not given, but it was sent to a friend from college who was the sister of an Edinburgh based Doctor. The necklace was said to be made from blue beads, which had turned green through age, as it had come from an Egyptian tomb and was believed to be around 3,000 years old.

View over Loch Leven

Whenever the necklace was held, it was said to feel like it was alive, moving like a snake, resulting in no one wanting to wear it, or even have it in their possession. With it laid aside in a safe place, over time the owner forgot all about it until a few years later when she found it while searching through her belongings. Remembering how the necklace had made her feel, and considering it to have no value given that she had never worn it and had forgotten she even had it, she quickly threw it into the waste paper bin to be disposed of.

Late that evening while she prepared for bed, she reached down to pick up her slippers that were beside the waste paper basket, and felt a freezing cold hand reach out and grab her by the wrist. She rationalised that she was tired and imagining things, but suddenly she heard noises coming from the basket. She describes it as being like something that was moving quickly around inside it and, thinking there was a mouse, she picked it up to check it yet found nothing there other than some waste paper and the necklace.

Fear set in as she remembered about the feeling of the necklace wriggling in her hands, and she put the bin outside her door before telling her brother about the incidents. Curious, he took the necklace and kept it in his bedroom, yet for the next few nights, his sleep was continuously disturbed by strange and unexplained noises.

They passed the necklace onto journalist and author, J W Herries, who had heard about its story and was keen to experiment with it. As he sat in his study examining the necklace, he heard the rustling noise similar to a mouse running around in paper, as described to him. When he went to look to see where it was coming from, the noise stopped and was replaced by knocking noises coming from his sideboard. When he went to check that, again the noise stopped, and was replaced by the sound of footsteps as though someone was walking down the hallway. Needless to say, when he checked, no one was there and again the noise moved, this time back to the sideboard.

Herries was keen to see if anyone else would witness such experiences, and took the necklace to his bedroom where his wife was just going to sleep. Without saying anything, he placed the necklace on her dressing table, and went to bed himself. Before he could do so, the light in the room started to dim before going back to full brightness. This repeated several times until he eventually switched it off. Throughout the night, he was awoken by knocking sounds coming from both the dressing table and the mirror above it, and although his wife was not disturbed through the night, she was terrified the following day when carrying a heavy iron griddle pan across the kitchen, and suddenly a loud knocking sound came from it. Herries kept the necklace for a week, during which time he documented all types of unexplained noises throughout the house, before he returned it to the doctor in Edinburgh.

When it arrived through the post, the doctor was just leaving for a trip to Loch Leven, and so put the envelope containing the necklace in his pocket. It was on his mind throughout the trip, his sister had made it clear he was to keep it in his room as she did not want it back, yet he was mindful of his own experiences with it, along with the encounters J W Herries and others had while in possession of the seemingly cursed necklace. Knowing he needed to rid himself and his family of it, he threw it overboard into the Loch Leven.

The case was later examined by Sir Arthur Conan Doyle, the famous creator of Sherlock Homes who, having considered all of the evidence, concluded that the strange occurrences were as a result of Egyptian occult power connected to the necklace. The necklace has never been recovered, and who knows what energy it is putting out within the waters of the loch.

About Scottish Paranormal

Scottish Paranormal is one of the oldest paranormal research teams in Scotland with a primary aim to document, and hopefully scientifically prove the existence of the paranormal. We are a serious group of professionally-minded adults who believe that skepticism is healthy, and that all reasonable explanations should be ruled out prior to declaring an experience to be paranormal in nature. we use both simple and high-tech electronic equipment to document and substantiate our experiences.

We are also heavily history based, we firmly believe that for there to be a reported haunting, there has to be a reason, and we will research the records to find both the historical accounts, and the earliest reports of the alleged haunting.

Within the team, we have 3 published authors of both historical and paranormal books, and 2 of our members have appeared on mainstream, television shows. You can follow us on Facebook by looking for **Scottish Paranormal** and we also operate **Haunted Scotland**, where we release detailed documentaries of our investigation work. Other Scottish Paranormal titles include:

The Unseen World: Afterlife Research
The Haunted Scotland Cookbook
Witch Memorials of Scotland

Printed in Great Britain
by Amazon